THIS IS ME!

ACROSTICS

Marvellous Poets

Edited By Sara Little

First published in Great Britain in 2022 by:

 Young**Writers** Est. 1991

Young Writers
Remus House
Coltsfoot Drive
Peterborough
PE2 9BF
Telephone: 01733 890066
Website: www.youngwriters.co.uk

Printed and bound in the UK by BookPrintingUK
Website: www.bookprintinguk.com
YB0509T

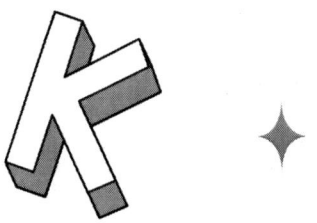

Foreword

Welcome Reader,

For Young Writers' latest competition *This Is Me Acrostics*, we asked primary school pupils to look inside themselves, to think about what makes them unique, and then write an acrostic poem about it! They rose to the challenge magnificently and the result is this fantastic collection of poems, celebrating them and the things that are important to them.

Here at Young Writers our aim is to encourage creativity in children and to inspire a love of the written word, so it's great to get such an amazing response, with some absolutely fantastic poems. It's important for children to focus on and celebrate themselves and this competition allowed them to write freely and honestly, celebrating what makes them great, expressing their hopes and fears, or simply writing about their favourite things. *This Is Me Acrostics* gave them the power of words.

I'd like to congratulate all the young poets in this anthology, I hope this inspires them to continue with their creative writing.

Contents

Theo Thomson (6) — 51
Jude Mckinnell (5) — 52
Leo Lawson (6) — 53
Ellis Easson (6) — 54
Polina Stasiukevic (7) — 55
Arabella Walker (5) — 56

New Horizons School, St Leonards-On-Sea

Cody Cook (6) — 57
Jude Dixon (5) — 58
Kyle Bristow (7) — 59
Harbin Palmer (6) — 60

Phoenix St Peter Academy, Lowestoft

Arlo Clarke (7) — 61
Elsie Belson (6) — 62
Sam Atkins (6) — 63
Beatrix Gillings (7) — 64
Gracie Woodrow (6) — 65
Bailey Salgado (7) — 66
Charlie Morgan (7) — 67
Kingsleigh Baker (6) — 68
Emily Morgan (7) — 69
Lily Fletcher (6) — 70

St Michael & All Angels CE Primary School, Rearsby

Jaiden Mistry (7) — 71
Summer Saunders (7) — 72
Alivia Turner (6) — 73
Olivia Hastings (7) — 74
Avni Patel (7) — 75
Prabhjot Varaiteh (7) — 76
Jax Stone (7) — 77
Phoebe Nolan (7) — 78
Lola Poppy Darson (6) — 79

Temple Learning Academy, Halton Moor

Harper-Raine Towers (7) — 80
Frankie Doughty (7) — 81
Mario Ciocilteu (6) — 82
Dani-Leigh Armitage (6) — 83
Callum Brownsett (7) — 84
Kishaun Greaves (7) — 85
Bobby Hudson (7) — 86
Archie Brown (7) — 87
Shane Ayeh (7) — 88
Layla Smith (6) — 89
Kaycee O'Nions (6) — 90

The Pilgrim School, Borstal

Jack Cumbers (6) — 91
Sonny Relf (7) — 92
Jamie Harris (6) — 93
Phoebe Jamil (7) — 94
Jessica Swain (6) — 95
Reeha Bhatti (6) — 96
Elsie Dorman (7) — 97
Brooke Parish (7) — 98
Capriah Taylor (6) — 99
Ruby Wright (6) — 100
Chlöe Toogood (6) — 101
Evelyn (6) — 102
Emily Hewing (6) — 103
Lilac Lockyer (6) — 104
Holly Shepherd (7) — 105
Leah Louise Sawyer Stannard (7) — 106
Dylan Gonzalo-Apolinario (7) — 107
Lily Gayner (6) — 108
Felix Fuller (6) — 109

Walker Memorial Primary School, Castlecaulfield

Logan Reid (7) — 110
Sam Kirkland (6) — 111
Harry Camley (5) — 112

William MacGregor Primary School, Tamworth

The Acrostics

My First Acrostic

T hey like to eat carrots,
O n the rocks,
R ough shell,
T hey are slow,
O n the grass,
I nside their shell,
S afe in their shell,
E veryone is feeding them,
S pinach is their favourite food.

Luke Chapman (10)

Pokémon, Yay!

P okémon Shield games,
O ak Wood is very dark in the game,
K eep Pokémon then they evolve,
É very Pokémon is a different type,
M y starter Pokémon was Scorbunny,
O n the game your character is Ash,
N o Pokémon is a lava type.

Joshua Farley (6)
Aldourie Primary School, Aldourie

The Tortoises

T hey like to eat carrots,
O n the rocks,
R ough shell,
T hey are slow,
O n the grass,
I nside their shell,
S afe in their shell,
E veryone is feeding them,
S pinach is their favourite food.

Ruairi Watson-McHardy (6)
Aldourie Primary School, Aldourie

Splash

S wimming is fun
W ater is hot
I can jump in the pool
M aking bubbles
M y swimming suit
I like to splash
N ice hot water
G ulping water.

Hallie Fraser (6)

Aldourie Primary School, Aldourie

Cats

C hase their tails in a circle
A cat likes to rest
T ails are soft
S leeping on the couch.

William Munroe (6)
Aldourie Primary School, Aldourie

Shark

S wim in the water

H ave sharp teeth

A ngry

R eally angry

K eep eating fish.

Kevin Griffiths (5)

Aldourie Primary School, Aldourie

Big, Brilliant Brazil

B ig statue of Christ the Redeemer
R ainforests cover most of Brazil
A mazon is the biggest rainforest
Z oom to the top of the Sugar Loaf
I guazu Falls is a big waterfall
L ong Amazon river is the second largest river in the world.

Robin Britland (6)
Bamford Primary School, Bamford

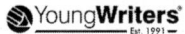

Unicorns

U nder the rainbow lives a unicorn

N ow and then everything seems normal

I n the wild, unicorns fly

C limb on me, said a unicorn

O ver and round the unicorns jump

R acing a unicorn is pretty hard

N ever touch a unicorn.

Dorothea Fowler (5)

Bamford Primary School, Bamford

My Brother

J oe is young,

O ur Joe and Hugo are good brothers,

S houting at dinner time,

E very day Joe is a cheeky monkey,

P laying with toys,

H elping is what Joe does.

Hugo Hope (6)
Bamford Primary School, Bamford

Football

F ootball is fun

O ver the goalkeeper

O ver into the goal

T eamwork

B alls get slide-tackled

A goal

L iking football

L ove it.

Freddie Hoggarth (6)
Bamford Primary School, Bamford

Spring

S un in the sky

P lants grow

R oses are blooming

I nsects are waking up

N ature is amazing

G o and enjoy your springtime.

Beatrix Fowler (7)

Bamford Primary School, Bamford

Beach

B eautiful beach

E veryone playing

A mazing volleyball player

C olourful ocean

H elping people on the beach.

Sully Spencer (6)
Bamford Primary School, Bamford

Buffalo Bills

B ills are good
I am a big fan
L ook at the Bills
L ook at Josh Allen
S uper Bowl Bills.

Joshua Rutter (6)
Bamford Primary School, Bamford

Phil

P hil is my pet.

H e lives in a cage.

I t's my favourite animal.

L et's have fun with Phil.

Noah Barabas (7)

Bamford Primary School, Bamford

Joey

J ump and play

O ut on walkies

E very day he sleeps and snores

Y ummy food and water.

Robyn Hodgson (5)

Bamford Primary School, Bamford

Animals

A bird comes and it is eating my bread,

N obody touched the dog because they were scared.

I opened the door and there was my dog and cat.

M y chicken was flying everywhere and it spilt my drink!

A bug is on my foot and it flew off.

L ook, there are lots of bees and flies! Away!

S eagull is here and it has landed on the sand.

Amaya Ali (7)
Blakehill Primary School, Idle

Gymnast Girl

G ive 100%.

Y ou have fun.

M ove your body into different shapes.

N ow don't be late for class.

A nyone can be a gymnast.

S tretch your arms and legs.

T ime to have a drink.

I rene is my teacher.

C oncentration is important.

S tretch shape is my favourite.

Isla-Rae Yarrow (7)

Blakehill Primary School, Idle

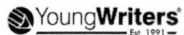
Creative

C olouring makes me happy.
R unning makes me hot.
E very day I enjoy school.
A pples are my favourite fruit.
T eal is my favourite colour.
I love being creative.
V alentine's day is my favourite holiday.
E ach day I do something creative at home.

Harveen Romana (6)
Blakehill Primary School, Idle

Rainbow Days

R ed is the first colour

A lways makes me happy

I can see it with my eyes

N o rainbow stays

B lue is the colour of the sky

O ver the houses they go

W ater from the rain helps them grow

S o beautiful.

Emilia Censani (6)
Blakehill Primary School, Idle

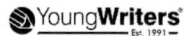

The Happy World

H aving a party is so much fun,
A new toy is really exciting!
P izza is really nice to eat,
P laying with my friends is joyful,
Y oghurts are my favourite, and so are you.

Emma Hyde (6)
Blakehill Primary School, Idle

Pandamonium

P layful panda!

A lways eating bamboo!

N ature is their home.

D angerous but cute!

A nd I love them so much!

Phoebe Flack (7) & Star

Blakehill Primary School, Idle

This Is Me

F ox class is the best.

R ight all the time.

I am always honest.

E xcellent me.

N ever rude.

D elicate with things.

L iterally amazing at writing.

Y es, I like myself.

A lways helpful and kind.

N othing is my favourite.

D ancing, I am good at.

S tar player.

P ractising a lot.

O lympic player.

R eally good at football.

T oo good at sport.

Y es, this is me.

Sophia Dexter (7)

Great Barton Primary Academy, Great Barton

This Is Me

T ummy grumbles when I'm hungry

H appy me

I sla is my name

S uperstars at school.

I love my family

S wimming is my favourite sport.

M y family is very kind.

E veryone in my family loves me.

Isla Moss (7)
Great Barton Primary Academy, Great Barton

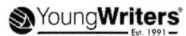

This Is Me

T his is my poem.
H ow do I eat?
I like ice cream.
S unny days are my favourite days.

I am excellent.
S pecial friends love me.

M y best friend is Noah.
E veryone loves me in my family.

Adelaide Emsden (6)
Great Barton Primary Academy, Great Barton

This Is Me

T offy is a pony

H orse riding

I am excellent

S tewee is my favourite toy.

I love pizza

S paghetti is my favourite food.

M y best friend is Clive

E xtraordinary Harriett.

Harriett Doidge (7)
Great Barton Primary Academy, Great Barton

This Is Me!

T ea time
H aving pasta
I s nice
S isters are the best.

I love my sister
S uper kind.

M y mummy is nice.
E at all my dinner.

Amelia Ranns (7)
Great Barton Primary Academy, Great Barton

William

W inter is the best.

I ndestructible brain.

L ove maths.

L ove reading.

I pswich is the best.

A wesome skateboarder.

M arvellous friend.

William Cole (7)

Great Barton Primary Academy, Great Barton

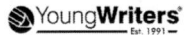

How I'm Sporty

S uper footballer
P erfect writer
O lympics is what I like to watch
R eigning world champion of football
T errific swimmer
Y ou are my manager.

Logan Hooker (7)
Great Barton Primary Academy, Great Barton

Joseph

J oseph is my name
O ften like my brother
S amuel is my brother
E xcited when Christmas comes
P erfect friend
H elpful person.

Joseph Atwell (7)
Great Barton Primary Academy, Great Barton

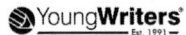

Rainbow

R aining

A mazing

I love purple

N ever-ending

B eautiful rainbow

O n fire

W ow, that's good colouring.

Dexie-Rae Runce (7)
Great Barton Primary Academy, Great Barton

Koala

K oalas are my favourite animals.
O ften they drink.
A lways eat eucalyptus.
L ovely koala.
A lways climbs up trees.

Tabatha-Lily Tate (6)
Great Barton Primary Academy, Great Barton

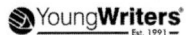

Freddie's Favourites

F reddie is my name.

R unning is my favourite thing to do on the field.

E ating my favourite cheese pizza.

D oing my reading.

Freddie Foreman (6)

Great Barton Primary Academy, Great Barton

My Favourite Dinosaur

R apid movers.

A n evil predator.

P erky all day.

T ypical hunter.

O bvious actions.

R aptor family.

Henry Lord (6)

Great Barton Primary Academy, Great Barton

Finley

F inley is kind.

I ncredibly affectionate.

N ever mean.

L oves numbers.

E nergetic.

Y oung man.

Finley Francis (7)

Great Barton Primary Academy, Great Barton

Blake

B eing kind.

L ooking after my cats.

A lways go to Duxford.

K ool Spitfires.

E xcellent at exercise.

Blake Pointon (6)

Great Barton Primary Academy, Great Barton

Toffy

T offy, my pony, is cheeky
O n the grass she eats
F unny, cute
F avourite pony
Y ucky food.

Claudia Doidge (7)
Great Barton Primary Academy, Great Barton

Sebby

S urfing dude
E xcellent at swimming
B athtime is fun
B ed is lovely
Y oghurts are yummy.

Sebby Mayes (6)

Great Barton Primary Academy, Great Barton

My Name

N othing frightens me
O h, I love my house
A ndy programmes are my favourite
H as a girlfriend.

Noah Steward (6)

Great Barton Primary Academy, Great Barton

My Life

R aif likes rattlesnakes

A corns falling down

I gloos are fun to make

F rosties ice cream.

Raif Worger (7)
Great Barton Primary Academy, Great Barton

This Is Elsie

E lsie
L oves her pet
S he is helpful
I love my hamster
E xcellent friend.

Elsie Humphreys (6)
Great Barton Primary Academy, Great Barton

Tiger

T igers are amazing
I n caves
G ood hunters
E ating meat
R eally fierce.

Lily-Jane Hayhoe (7)
Great Barton Primary Academy, Great Barton

Archie

A nimals

R oblox

C risps

H orses

I am cool

E xtremely cool.

Archie Hayhoe (7)

Great Barton Primary Academy, Great Barton

Oreo, My Cat

O reo likes our bedroom
R eally cheeky
E veryone loves Oreos
O range cat biscuits.

Tee-Jay Bedford (6)
Great Barton Primary Academy, Great Barton

My Name

C aring to everyone
L ikes pizza
I like Roblox
V ery kind
E nergetic.

Clive Morgan (7)
Great Barton Primary Academy, Great Barton

Mason

M ason is good
A dventurous
S kilful
O nline all the time
N ice.

Mason Hutchingson (7)
Great Barton Primary Academy, Great Barton

Fox Class

F ox class is my favourite

O reos are yummy

E **X** ercising is fun.

Courtney Johnson (7)
Great Barton Primary Academy, Great Barton

Austin's Poem

A utumn is when my birthday is, when the tree leaves change to beautiful colours.

U nder the duvet is where I hide from my brothers when we play hide-and-seek.

S panish club is after school on Monday. When it's time to go home, I say, "Adios amigos!"

T rampolining makes me happy, it's fun when I bounce up high in the air.

I nside out, shake it all about - I've got all the dance moves!

N ow I wear glasses. They make me look really smart.

Austin Walker (6)

Mount Nod Primary School, Coventry

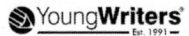

This Is Me: Caleb Mills

T rees are fun to climb

H aving sweets on film night

I ce cream is yummy

S ucks to be a pudding because I eat all of it!

I love Grogu

S onny (my nan's dog) is the best.

"M om, can I have my tablet?"

E dan (my brother) is on his mission and I miss him!

Caleb Mills (6)

Mount Nod Primary School, Coventry

Elena-Rose

E lena is my name
L aughing is so much fun
E veryone should do it
N ow let's play in the sun
A fter we put on suncream.

R olling on the grass
O n a sunny day
S miling makes me happy
E very time I play.

Elena-Rose Aubrey (6)
Mount Nod Primary School, Coventry

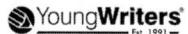

This Is Me

A mazing writer,
N ice and kind,
N ow let's see,
A lways understanding.

G ood and generous,
R eally working hard,
A sking questions,
C ontributing in lessons,
E xciting girl.

Anna Jones (7)
Mount Nod Primary School, Coventry

Penguin

P enguins dive down

E ven when it is cold

N ighttime they go into their cave

G oing to eat some fish

U p they swim to the surface

I nto the ice

N ext, they went to penguin island.

Theo Thomson (6)

Mount Nod Primary School, Coventry

Football

F riends playing matches
O utside getting exercise
O ffside rules
T eam players
B est sport ever
A lways passing to my teammates
L et's have fun
L ots of goals.

Jude Mckinnell (5)
Mount Nod Primary School, Coventry

About My Mommy

M ommy helps me to read my book

O n my table my mommy, daddy, and sister
sit

M y favourite part of my mommy is she
plays games

M onday my mommy puts me to bed

Y ummy food that my mommy does.

Leo Lawson (6)

Mount Nod Primary School, Coventry

Soccer

S occer Tots was my first football team
O wning the field, scoring goals
C heering my team
C lap and cheer
E veryone on my team
R acing up and down the pitch.

This is me.

Ellis Easson (6)
Mount Nod Primary School, Coventry

Party

P laying in the Wacky Warehouse,
A lot of children jumping up and down,
R unning around on the squishy mats,
T ime for the birthday cake!
"Y es!" shouted everyone.

Polina Stasiukevic (7)
Mount Nod Primary School, Coventry

Dogs

D ogs are my favourite animal
O ver the fence, I saw a dog
G oing for a walk in the field
S wimming puppies in the lake.

Arabella Walker (5)

Mount Nod Primary School, Coventry

Amazing

A lice in Wonderland is the best
M usic, singing, and the rest
A riel is a favourite, too
Z ootropolis and the colour blue
I am helpful, and really cool
N ever naughty when at school
G irls and boys rule!

Cody Cook (6)
New Horizons School, St Leonards-On-Sea

I Am Jude

I am Jude.

A nd I am a cool dude.
M y kittens are cute.

J et's a real beaut.
U nder the water I swim.
D ive like a fish with a fin.
E very week I can't wait to get in.

Jude Dixon (5)

New Horizons School, St Leonards-On-Sea

This Is Me

T he name is Kyle
H elping is my style
I am a twin
S wimming is my thing.

I love Halloween
S pooky and mean.

M int chocolate is great
E veryone's my mate.

Kyle Bristow (7)
New Horizons School, St Leonards-On-Sea

Harbin

H appy
A nd cheeky
R eady to play
B right and clever
I n every way
N o one else is quite...

... Like me.

Harbin Palmer (6)
New Horizons School, St Leonards-On-Sea

Gardening

G ood at reading.

A super-duper puppy!

R eally crazy and silly.

D elicious pizza!

E njoying a bit.

N ice and warm inside the house.

I ncredible at making stuff

N ever super-duper naughty.

G ardening is the best.

Arlo Clarke (7)

Phoenix St Peter Academy, Lowestoft

This Is Me

T oys are really fun to play with.
H ave lots of fun with friends.
I love dogs.
S weet, I am.

I like to eat fish nuggets.
S ongs, I love listening to.

M y eyes are brown.
E xcellent at maths.

Elsie Belson (6)

Phoenix St Peter Academy, Lowestoft

Sam Atkins

S nakes are the best.
A mazing at maths.
M aths is the best.

A mazing at crafting.
T ikTok is the best.
K ind to my friends.
I nsects are small.
N ever give up.
S uper son.

Sam Atkins (6)

Phoenix St Peter Academy, Lowestoft

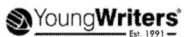

Beatrix

B uzzing with energy
E xcited for trips
A dventurous on adventures
T otally love fashion
R eady to have fun!
I like baguettes
X -ray vision to see how you are feeling.

Beatrix Gillings (7)

Phoenix St Peter Academy, Lowestoft

This Is Me

G reat at art

R eally kind

A pple picking

C lever at helping

I like being kind

E cho is my favourite.

W orld's best BFF is Brooke.

Gracie Woodrow (6)

Phoenix St Peter Academy, Lowestoft

Bailey

B rilliant at watching TV.

A imee is my sister.

I am seven.

L ove Minecraft, gold, and diamonds.

E asy to play Minecraft.

Y ellow.

Bailey Salgado (7)

Phoenix St Peter Academy, Lowestoft

Charlie

C aring and kind

H ungry all the time

A utism

R onnie is cute

L ove going to the park

I am seven

E lephant love.

Charlie Morgan (7)
Phoenix St Peter Academy, Lowestoft

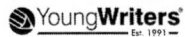

Sport

S uper at dodgeball
P laying to get better
O riginal me in PE
R eally good at football
T rying my best in PE and tournaments.

Kingsleigh Baker (6)

Phoenix St Peter Academy, Lowestoft

Emily

E ating chocolate pancakes
M arvellous as school work
I love drawing
L ove school
Y oghurt is my favourite food.

Emily Morgan (7)
Phoenix St Peter Academy, Lowestoft

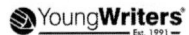

Lily

L ove pizza

I am Lily

L ove my family

Y ummy McDonald's and pizza.

Lily Fletcher (6)

Phoenix St Peter Academy, Lowestoft

Creative

C ats are adorable and they can run so fast.

R elaxing is very comfortable on a comfy, cosy chair.

E aster hunt is so fun because you get lots of chocolate.

A seagull always steals my fish and chips.

T ons of times I get too excited.

I love my two cats, my three dogs, and my mummy.

V ery creative, that's what I like to do.

E very day I am super creative, I like making lots of stuff.

Jaiden Mistry (7)

St Michael & All Angels CE Primary School, Rearsby

Horse Riding

H appy, hard, and careful.
O ut taking care of horses.
R ock star at horse riding.
S kilful at cantering.
E xtremely happy.

R adiantly fast.
I nteresting and fun.
D ifficult, dangerous.
I ntelligently fun and crazy.
N ice and fun.
G raceful every day.

Summer Saunders (7)

St Michael & All Angels CE Primary School, Rearsby

My Mermaid

M y mermaid is happy today.

"E xcellent work," said the teacher.

"R ight, this is your last chance."

M y last day today.

A ctually, it is my first day.

I am scared today.

D emonstrate your act for the show.

Alivia Turner (6)

St Michael & All Angels CE Primary School, Rearsby

Scooter

S cooters are scary.

C rossing roads.

O ver the hill with my friends.

O ver playing with my friends

T iredly I start to get tired, so I stop.

E xcited.

R iding my scooter is fun.

Olivia Hastings (7)

St Michael & All Angels CE Primary School, Rearsby

Craft

C ute unicorns make me laugh

R ed paint for love hearts

A lways making new things

F unny animals to make

T errific craft is my hobby.

Avni Patel (7)
St Michael & All Angels CE Primary School, Rearsby

Dancing

D ancing is my hobby
A lways like to dance
N ice to go around the house
C arefully I dance
E xultantly I move on the smooth floor.

Prabhjot Varaiteh (7)
St Michael & All Angels CE Primary School, Rearsby

Fossil Fun

F ossil fun
O n a gleaming hot day
S hining at me
S o hot, it is so hot
I t will be the end
L ast fossil!

Jax Stone (7)

St Michael & All Angels CE Primary School, Rearsby

Love

L lamas are my favourite.

O ranges are so pretty.

V ery well in my maths.

E ggs cracked open when I just broke them.

Phoebe Nolan (7)

St Michael & All Angels CE Primary School, Rearsby

I Love Yoga

Y ou can stretch and breathe

O n my glittery mat

G oing to my lesson

A lways make shapes with my body.

Lola Poppy Barson (6)

St Michael & All Angels CE Primary School, Rearsby

Harper-Raine

H appy Harper-Raine
A mazing
R eady for anything
P lays and
E verything's easy
R eally fun and active.
-
R eally
A rty
I like playing with my friends
N ice dog walker
E xciting.

Harper-Raine Towers (7)
Temple Learning Academy, Halton Moor

Frankie

F riendly guy
R aw says the best person
A rgh I nearly had a heart attack
N ow I know my maths
K now where to go
I know what I need
E ggs are my favourite.

Frankie Doughty (7)
Temple Learning Academy, Halton Moor

Mario

M ost friendly with friends.

A mazing with maths.

R esponsible with my sister.

I always run rapidly in the playground.

O utstanding goalkeeper.

Mario Ciocilteu (6)

Temple Learning Academy, Halton Moor

Dani-Leigh

D rawing

A mazing

N ice

I nteresting.

-

L ovely

E xcellent

I love dogs

G ood

H appy.

Dani-Leigh Armitage (6)
Temple Learning Academy, Halton Moor

Amazing Callum

C ute smile and creative.

A nimal lover.

L oving family.

L earning is fun.

U nbelievable.

M agnificent work from me.

Callum Brownsett (7)

Temple Learning Academy, Halton Moor

Kishaun

K ind

I am kind

S o happy

H e drank too much cocoa

A funny boy

U nbelievable

N ame is Kishaun.

Kishaun Greaves (7)

Temple Learning Academy, Halton Moor

Bobby

B eautiful handwriting.

O utstanding.

B iggest smile in the class.

B eaver of the week.

Y ay, I make everybody smile.

Bobby Hudson (7)

Temple Learning Academy, Halton Moor

Archie

A mazing at art
R eally cool
C ares for his friends
H elps out there
I am awesome
E ats chocolate.

Archie Brown (7)

Temple Learning Academy, Halton Moor

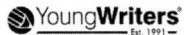

Shane

S uper and amazing
H appy and hardworking
A mazing and talented
N ice and caring
E xcellent and exciting.

Shane Ayeh (7)
Temple Learning Academy, Halton Moor

About Me

L oving family.

A mazing friend.

Y ou are talented.

L ikes drawing.

A mazing writing.

Layla Smith (6)

Temple Learning Academy, Halton Moor

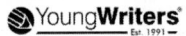

Kaycee

K ind friend

A ce

Y ou

C ool

E xcellent

E xciting.

Kaycee O'Nions (6)

Temple Learning Academy, Halton Moor

This Is Me

J elly, the YouTuber, is my thing,
A ll types of animals too,
C ristiano Ronaldo is my fave,
K indness comes easily to me.

B uilding makes me happy,
E ach friend of mine does too,
N ella, my sister, is the best in the world.

C rabbing makes me carefree,
U nited are mine and Dad's team,
M cDonald's is yummy to me,
B each days with my family,
E xcited to start weight-lifting with mum,
R eptiles don't scare me,
S pider-Man is another name for me.

Jack Cumbers (6)
The Pilgrim School, Borstal

Sonny And Kitty

S pain is my favourite place
O nce I saw a real axolotl
N ew forest is great
N ow I'm going on the trampoline
Y ou are my perfect mum.

A nts are my pets
N intendos are perfect
D ad gives me lots of hugs.

K itty is my cat baby
I want to be a Ghostbuster
T een Titans Go! is really funny
T he basking shark only eats plankton
Y ay, it's Christmas!

Sonny Relf (7)

The Pilgrim School, Borstal

Cats In Love

C urling up in a ball,
A ll day long she cleans her furry coat
T o make it fluffy and clean.
S he likes to sit on my homework, or...

I n my bed!
N ow, she's meowing for more food!

L ots of sharp claws in her paws.
O n her own she likes to be...
V ery naughty and scratches the sofa!
E very day she purrs, and I love her.

Jamie Harris (6)
The Pilgrim School, Borstal

Phoebe J

P alaeontology I want to do
H airstyling and reading are fun
O n Friday we have family movie nights
E lephants and Bear-Bear, I snuggle with them at night
B est friends with Anoushka and Kadie
E verything above makes me Phoebe...

J amil.

Phoebe Jamil (7)
The Pilgrim School, Borstal

Magical

M eeting the queen is my dream.
A dancer is what I want to be.
G ymnastics is as fun as the sun.
I t is amazing when I bake a cake.
C ome in the snow, it's a blast.
A pples and oranges are the best.
L aughing is so good.

Jessica Swain (6)
The Pilgrim School, Borstal

Humanity

H elping others
U nderstanding everyone
M aking someone smile
A kind word is charity
N ever forget God's creations
I t makes a better Earth
T he world is full of love
Y ou will find peace.

Reeha Bhatti (6)
The Pilgrim School, Borstal

Happy Hamster

H appy hamster

A lways having fun

M y hamster licks me and ice cream

S afe and sound in her bed

T ickling her sister with her whiskers

E asy to carry around

R unning around and around on her wheel.

Elsie Dorman (7)
The Pilgrim School, Borstal

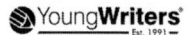

Why I Like My iPad

I like my iPad because it's all mine.

P eople always compete for the TV remote

A nd because I have my iPad I don't have to, haha

D addy's not allowed to watch my iPad because it's all mine.

Brooke Parish (7)

The Pilgrim School, Borstal

Happy

H appy is what I like to be

A s happy as a bird in a tree

P lease be polite and always nice

P rotect all creatures, even mice

Y our kindness is free, just like honey from a bee.

Capriah Taylor (6)
The Pilgrim School, Borstal

Ruby Wright

R ed

U nique

B eautiful

Y ellow.

W onderful

R espectful

I ntelligent

G rateful

H elpful

T alented.

Ruby Wright (6)

The Pilgrim School, Borstal

Chloe

C hloe loves scootering in the park.

H as a rainbow unicorn called Melody.

L oves her mummy.

O n and off her bike she goes.

E very Friday Chloe goes swimming.

Chlöe Toogood (6)

The Pilgrim School, Borstal

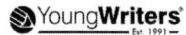

Family

F riends are funny
A melia is my favourite cousin
M ummy is beautiful
I ncredible nannies
L ovely family makes me happy
Y ummy food in my tummy.

Evelyn (6)

The Pilgrim School, Borstal

All About Me

E very day I sing and dance.
M ake-up I wear at the weekend.
I like playing football.
L ittle Mix is my favourite band.
Y es, I like purple.

Emily Hewing (6)
The Pilgrim School, Borstal

Lilac

L ots of fun days off
I like to swim and draw
L eaping on the trampoline
A nd spending time with family
C rab gymnastics on the floor.

Lilac Lockyer (6)
The Pilgrim School, Borstal

Holly

H appy and helpful all the time.

O ne of a kind.

L ovely and caring.

L oveable and sweet.

Y ep, that's me!

Holly Shepherd (7)

The Pilgrim School, Borstal

Mummy

M akes nice food.

U ses make-up.

M um looks good.

M um changes her hair.

Y ou make me smile.

Leah Louise Sawyer Stannard (7)

The Pilgrim School, Borstal

Ball

B oys playing basketball,
A nyone can take a shot,
L ikes any ball game,
L oves playing with friends.

Dylan Gonzalo-Apolinario (7)
The Pilgrim School, Borstal

Dance

D ate in the morning
A nimals in music
N eed the music
C ats are cute
E dwin is my brother.

Lily Gayner (6)
The Pilgrim School, Borstal

Lovely Llamas

L ovely llamas
L ive in South America
A lpacas are not llamas
M y favourite
A nimal.

Felix Fuller (6)
The Pilgrim School, Borstal

Scotland

S cotland beach, I love it.

C ountry of fun.

O ctopus in the sea.

T ower up high

L and is low, the sky is high.

A untie Christine is lots of fun.

N ice people.

D riving onto the boat.

Logan Reid (7)

Walker Memorial Primary School, Castlecaulfield

Fireman

F ires are dangerous
I will
R ing 999
E mergency, come quick!
M y dad is a fireman
A mbulance comes too
N ow we are safe.

Sam Kirkland (6)
Walker Memorial Primary School, Castlecaulfield

Animals

A nts run
N ight owls hoot
I guanas creep
M onkeys climb
A lligators snap
L ions roar
S nakes hiss.

Harry Camley (5)
Walker Memorial Primary School, Castlecaulfield

Happy

H aving fun.

A lways smiling.

P laying in the playpark.

P laying with everyone.

Y es, all these things make me happy.

Jessica Graham (6)
Walker Memorial Primary School, Castlecaulfield

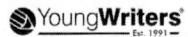

Family

F amily
A lways makes me smile
M ummy is kind
I love my dad
L ots of hugs
Y ou are safe.

Jack Gilmore-McMenemy (5)
Walker Memorial Primary School, Castlecaulfield

Dance

D ance party.

A pples growing on trees.

N urses help you.

C ute dogs.

E lephants at the zoo.

Cain Hamilton (6)

Walker Memorial Primary School, Castlecaulfield

Happy

H appy Harry
A lways sharing
P laying outside
P laying with my friends
Y ou make me happy.

Harry Kirkland (6)

Walker Memorial Primary School, Castlecaulfield

Spring

S unshine.

P lay outside.

R ainy days.

I feed the birds.

N ew animals are born.

G reen grass.

Liliana Drozd (7)
William MacGregor Primary School, Tamworth

Young Writers Information

We hope you have enjoyed reading this book – and that you will continue to in the coming years.

If you're the parent or family member of an enthusiastic poet or story writer, do visit **www.youngwriters.co.uk/subscribe** and sign up to receive news, competitions, writing challenges and tips, activities and much, much more! There's lots to keep budding writers motivated!

If you would like to order further copies of this book, or any of our other titles, then please give us a call or order via your online account.

Young Writers
Remus House
Coltsfoot Drive
Peterborough
PE2 9BF
(01733) 890066
info@youngwriters.co.uk

Join in the conversation!
Tips, news, giveaways and much more!

 **YoungWritersUK**  **YoungWritersCW**  **youngwriterscw**